What's Your Birthstone?

Did you know that each month of the year has a **birthstone?** A birthstone is a gem that has been assigned to a certain month to honor the birthdays of people born in that month. For example, April's birthstone is the diamond. Which is your birthstone?

Month	Birthstone
January	Garnet
February	Amethyst
March	Aquamarine
April	Diamond
May	Emerald
June	Alexandrite
July	Ruby
August	Peridot
September	Sapphire
October	Opal
November	Citrine
December	Blue Topaz

This chart names the traditional birthstones for each month of the year. Many people believe that wearing their birthstones brings good luck!

What Are Gemstones?

Most gems are formed from **minerals.** To become a gem, a mineral must cool and harden into a solid **crystal.** Crystals are hardened minerals that have special shapes and patterns.

When they are first discovered and **mined,** most gems look like ordinary rocks. They are often rough and unevenly shaped. In the hands of talented gem cutters, however, these raw chunks of mineral become **brilliant** gemstones. The best gemstones are often made into jewelry.

Gemstones are like snowflakes because no two are exactly the same. Gemstones come in every color of the rainbow, and when they are cut and polished, their colors sparkle and shine. The gemstones that sparkle and shine the most are worth the most money!

Rough diamond

Cut diamonds

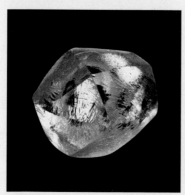

A Gem of a Tale!

by Donna Latham

PEARSON

Scott Foresman

Editorial Offices: Glenview, Illinois • Parsippany, New Jersey • New York, New York
Sales Offices: Needham, Massachusetts • Duluth, Georgia • Glenview, Illinois
Coppell, Texas • Ontario, California • Mesa, Arizona

ISBN: 0-328-13375-2

4 5 6 7 8 9 10 V0G1 14 13 12 11 10 09 08 07 06

These are some of the shapes into which gemstones are cut. Each cut, or shape, reflects light differently. Which cut is your favorite?

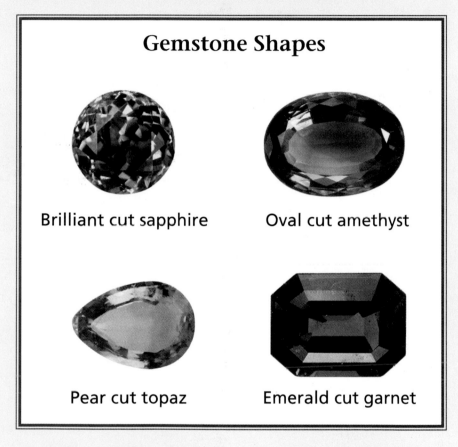

Gemstone Shapes

Brilliant cut sapphire

Oval cut amethyst

Pear cut topaz

Emerald cut garnet

Where in the world are gemstones found? Gemstones are found everywhere! Many gemstones are found here in the United States, and others are found thousands of miles away on different continents.

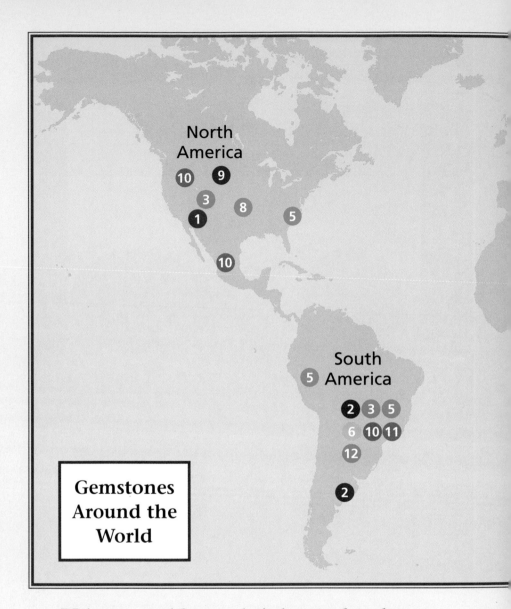

North America

South America

Gemstones Around the World

Using a world map, let's locate the places gemstones are found. We'll focus on the twelve gemstones that are used as birthstones.

Look at the map key to find the continents where each gemstone is mined. You will find the names of the countries where each gemstone is found as you read the following pages.

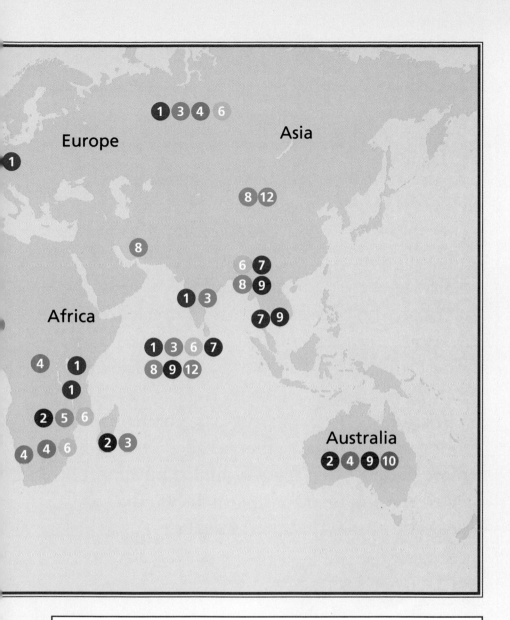

Europe

Asia

Africa

Australia

❶ Garnet	❼ Ruby
❷ Amethyst	❽ Peridot
❸ Aquamarine	❾ Sapphire
❹ Diamond	❿ Opal
❺ Emerald	⓫ Citrine
❻ Alexandrite	⓬ Blue Topaz

January • Garnet

When most people think of garnet, they picture a red-colored gem, and the most valuable garnets do have a rich, red color. But January's birthstone comes in every color except blue.

Garnet is found in the Czech Republic in Europe, in the Eurasian country Russia, and in the Asian countries India and Sri Lanka. Green garnet, which is rare, is found in two African countries, Kenya and Tanzania.

A kind of Arizona garnet has a name that sounds strange. This garnet is called the "anthill garnet" because it is actually mined by ants! The ants dig up soil to make their anthills, and the garnets are brought up to the surface.

Garnet's most common colors are red, lemon, tangerine, and brown. Green garnet is rare.

February • Amethyst

Amethyst is February's birthstone. It ranges in color from a very light lavender to a dark purple. The darkest kind of amethyst is found in Australia.

Amethyst is also mined in the South American countries Brazil and Uruguay and in the African countries Madagascar and Zambia.

Did you know that purple has long been considered the color of kings and queens? The British Crown Jewels, some of the most famous jewels anywhere, contain amethyst gemstones.

Can you find the amethyst gemstones in this photograph?

March • Aquamarine

March's birthstone is the aquamarine. Aquamarine is **transparent,** which means that light can pass through it.

Aquamarine means "seawater" in Latin, and aquamarine's light blue color makes it look like the sea. Some aquamarines have little green flecks, which make them look even more like the ocean. The most valuable aquamarine gemstones, however, are sky-blue in color.

Brazil is the world's best source of aquamarine, but it is also found in India, Madagascar, Sri Lanka, and Russia.

Here in the United States, aquamarine is mined in the state of Colorado. In fact, aquamarine is Colorado's state gem!

Rough aquamarines

April • Diamond

Diamond is nature's hardest material and the world's longest-lasting gem. Because of a diamond's hardness, almost nothing can wear it down. In fact, it can be cut only by another diamond.

The world's largest producer of diamond is Australia. Diamond is also mined in Russia and in three African countries, Congo, Namibia, and Botswana. On which two continents are both aquamarine and diamond mined? Use the map and map key on pages 6 and 7 to find out.

Colorless diamonds can split light into the colors of the rainbow.

May • Emerald

Did you know that some emeralds cost more than diamonds? It's true! Perfect emeralds are very rare. What makes a perfect emerald? Emeralds with a deep green color and no **flaws,** or defects, are rated best.

Can you guess why the emerald is North Carolina's state gem? Emeralds are mined there! **Rockhounds** are collectors who hunt for rocks that contain gems, and each year rockhounds come to North Carolina from all over the United States to dig for emeralds!

Where else in the world is emerald found? Colombia, in South America, mines most of the world's emeralds. They are also mined in Brazil and Zambia.

Emeralds are mined in North Carolina.

June • Alexandrite

Alexandrite is June's birthstone. This green stone was first discovered in Russia in 1830. It was named after Prince Alexander, who would later become Alexander II, emperor of Russia.

When moved from sunlight to artificial lighting, Alexandrite changes from green to reddish-purple. This makes it very valuable!

Today, Brazil mines the greatest amount of alexandrite. It is also found in Sri Lanka and Myanmar in Southeast Asia. Zambia and another African country, Zimbabwe, produce some too. On which two continents are both emerald and alexandrite found?

Emperor
Alexander II
of Russia

July • Ruby

July's birthstone is the ruby. It has a deep, glowing, red color and is very hard. Only diamond is harder. Ruby is one of the most valuable of all gems, and it is very rare. Rubies that are pure red with a tiny amount of blue are rarer than any. These crimson-colored rubies are known as pigeon's blood, and they are incredibly expensive!

Most rubies come from Myanmar, Burma, Thailand, and Sri Lanka, all countries in Southeast Asia.

A master jeweler cleans the British Crown Jewels.

August • Peridot

Peridot is the birthstone for August. Peridot, like aquamarine, is transparent, and most peridots have a light green or greenish-yellow color. Iron, a metal found deep in Earth, gives peridot its green-yellow color.

Peridot reaches Earth's surface through volcanic eruptions, but peridot has also come from outer space. Pieces of peridot have been found in meteors that have crashed into Earth!

Peridot is mined in the Asian countries Pakistan, Myanmar, China, and Sri Lanka. But most peridot is mined in the United States.

The iron in peridot gives the gem its green color.

September • Sapphire

September's birthstone is the sapphire. Like aquamarine and peridot, sapphire is transparent. Hard and rare, sapphire comes in many colors including violet, orange, and green. Blue sapphires, however, are the most valuable.

Star sapphires are special sapphires that reflect six points of light. When a star sapphire is placed beneath light, a star seems to flicker inside it.

Sapphires are mined in Thailand, Myanmar, Sri Lanka, and Australia. In the United States they are found in Montana.

A sapphire mine on the island of Madagascar

October • Opal

Opal is October's birthstone. Opal can be blue, green, black, or white. When an opal is moved from side to side, it sparkles with the colors of the rainbow.

Australia mines the greatest number of opals—and the most valuable ones. Smaller amounts of opal are found in Brazil and in Mexico, our neighbor to the south. In the United States, opals are mined in Idaho, Oregon, and Nevada.

Mining opals in Australia

Opals reflect all the colors of the rainbow.

17

November • Citrine

November's birthstone is citrine. Citrine is formed from a type of colored **quartz.** Quartz is a transparent mineral. Citrine has qualities similar to those of amethyst. In fact, when amethyst is heated, it changes color and becomes citrine!

Citrine has a yellow color much like that of a lemon. Citrine's name comes from the French word *citron*, which means lemon!

Citrine also comes in shades of brown, gold, and orange, and like many other birthstones, it is transparent. Most citrine is mined in Brazil.

Citrine is one of these many gemstones mined in Brazil.

December • Blue Topaz

We've nearly finished describing all twelve birthstones! The last of the twelve birthstones is December's blue topaz. The blue topaz looks similar to aquamarine.

Most of the blue topaz that we see today has been treated with heat. When you treat a colorless topaz with heat, the topaz takes on a sky blue color.

Like the gemstone citrine, blue topaz is found in Brazil. It is also found in Sri Lanka, China, and the African country Nigeria.

Rough topaz

Famous Gemstones

Some gemstones have become world famous because of their great size and beauty.

The royal-blue Hope Diamond is one of the most famous gemstones ever. Unlike colorless diamonds, this special diamond has a beautiful violet color. You can see the Hope Diamond at the Smithsonian Museum in Washington, D.C.

Also on display at the Smithsonian Museum is the Roebling Opal, one of the world's largest opals. This opal is jet-black, with brilliant colors swirling inside it, and it weighs about a pound and a half! It was discovered in Nevada in 1917.

The Star of India is one of the largest blue star sapphires in the world. You can see it at New York's Museum of Natural History. It weighs about four ounces and is almost the size of a baseball!

We've now toured the world of gemstones. From garnet to blue topaz, and everything in between, you've learned just about everything there is to know about each of the twelve birthstones!

Many different gemstones are traded in Asia.

Now Try This

Dig Up Some Gemstone Facts!

The world's most popular and well-known gemstones are the twelve birthstones. However, there are many other interesting gemstones.

Scan over the list of gemstones in the box below. Then choose one to research. Use good reference sources, such as encyclopedias, library books, and the Internet, to find out about the gemstone you've chosen.

More Gemstones		
agate	amber	ametrine
bloodstone	coral	iolite
jade	jasper	kunzite
moonstone	onyx	pearl
tanzanite	tourmaline	turquoise

In your own words, write down some facts about your gemstone. Some good things to note are its color or colors, how rare it is, where it is mined, and any unusual facts.

When you have finished your fact sheet, try sketching your gemstone. Then make a colorful poster about your gemstone. Use the facts from your fact sheet and the drawing you have made to design your poster.

Finally, share your poster and the information you have learned with your classmates!

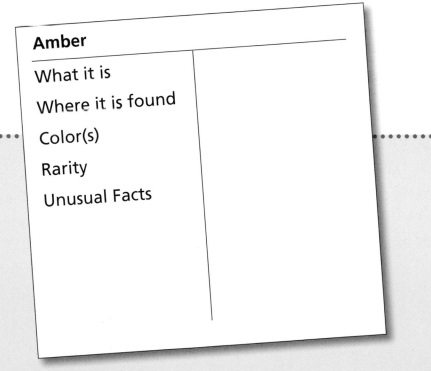

Amber

What it is

Where it is found

Color(s)

Rarity

Unusual Facts

Glossary

birthstone *n.* a gemstone associated with one of the twelve months of the year.

brilliant *adj.* very bright and shiny.

crystal *n.* a hard, solid piece of some substance that is naturally formed of flat surfaces and angles. Crystals can be small, like grains of salt, or large like some kinds of stone.

flaws *n.* in gems, defects or blemishes.

minerals *n.* solid substances, usually dug from Earth. Minerals often form crystals.

mined *v.* dug up from under the ground.

quartz *n.* a very hard mineral found in many different types of rock.

rockhounds *n.* the nickname given to people who hunt, dig, and collect rocks and gems.

transparent *adj.* allowing light to pass through.